Help Your Child S

Simple Strategies for Parents

Renaissance
Learning™

JA
372,13
KRA

Renaissance Learning
P.O. Box 45016
Madison, WI 53744-5016
(800) 200-4848

Printed in the United States of America

ISBN 1-893751-80-5

Writing by Kraft & Kraft
Editing by Dottie Raymer
Illustrations by George Sebok

Cover art Special thanks to the following artists for their drawings: Left top corner: Ingrid Klyve-Madden; Top row left to right: Timothy Hardie; Shireen Ramos; Francine Lease. Bottom row left to right: Elizabeth Santschi; Acadiarose McGovern; Spencer Campbell.

12/01

Contents

Introduction v

The Basic Six

1. Read to your child 2
2. Talk with your child 3
3. Establish a homework time 4
4. Limit TV time 6
5. Use these magic words 7
6. Visit the library regularly 8

Beyond the Basic Six

7. Use calendars for planning 10
8. Do quick math drills 14
9. Establish a family reading night 16
10. Put a bookshelf in your child's room 17
11. Put a reading basket in the bathroom 18
12. Give books as gifts 20
13. Take your child to a reading or story hour 21
14. Subscribe to a daily newspaper 22
15. Give your child a bed lamp 23
16. Don't be too eager to push your child
    beyond "easy" books 24
17. Limit extracurricular activities 25
18. Establish a school-night routine 28
19. Establish a school-morning routine 30
20. Make breakfast interesting 32

21. Get your child a clock 33
22. Create a study space 34
23. Buy your child a really cool pen 36
24. Give your child a dictionary 37
25. Buy a globe 38
26. Help your child get organized 39
27. Set up a family message center 42
28. Post a word of the day 44
29. Write letters 45
30. Clip coupons 46
31. Give your child a diary 47
32. Give your child a scrapbook 48
33. Play cards with your child 50
34. Play board games with your child 51
35. Play word games with your child 52
36. Teach math with money 53
37. Take monthly family field trips 54
38. Teach your child how to 55
39. Save your child's schoolwork 56
40. Find something to praise 57
41. Stay in touch with your child's teacher 58
42. Don't 59
43. Do 60
Six Books for Reading Aloud 61
Ten High-Interest Books That Are Easy to Read 62
Ten Stimulating Picture Books 63
Ten Chapter Books 64
Seven Books for You 65
Five Web Sites for You 66

Introduction

How can you help your child succeed in school? You can't tag along during the school day, of course, but you can provide help at home.

What help can you provide, and how can you possibly find the time to provide it?

This book answers those questions.

The key is establishing regular strategies and routines that lay a foundation for success.

As you consider the strategies that follow, remind yourself that families, children, and parents differ from one another. Choose the two strategies that you think will be easiest for you and your child to put into effect. Start with those. Add others when you can.

Each additional routine will bring your child closer to success.

The Basic Six

In this section, we've described six basic strategies for success. These are the most important routines that you could possibly adopt.

If you're wondering where to begin, start here. If you're thinking that you don't have much time to spare, start here. If you feel that your resources are very limited, start here.

If you do nothing more than establish these six routines as part of your child's learning life, you will have done a great deal. You will know that you are making a real difference in your child's chances of success.

1 Read to your child.

Reading aloud is *the* most effective routine to help your child succeed.

Make it a regular activity. Reading daily is best, but if you can't manage that, make it every other day. Bedtime is traditional, but it may not be best for you. Try reading while your child is in the bathtub or while she's waiting for the school bus to arrive.

Get your child involved in choosing the books that you read. Take her to a library or bookstore. Think of it as visiting a buffet. Encourage browsing and tasting.

If you and she find that a book you're reading is too hard, too easy, or not very interesting, drop it. If your child asks for the same book again and again, go right on reading it. The more pleasure she gets from reading, the more she'll want to read.

2 Talk with your child.

Conversation requires thinking as well as speaking. People who practice the art of conversation learn to voice their own ideas in their own words instead of just accepting and repeating what they've heard others say.

How can you get your child to start conversing? Ask a question that will get him thinking. Try some of these conversation starters (and be sure to join in the conversations they start):

- ◆ What do you think about . . . ?
- ◆ Which books would you take to a desert island?
- ◆ Which historical figure would you invite to dinner?
- ◆ Where would you go if you could visit any place on earth?
- ◆ What would you like to be remembered for?

3 Establish a homework time.

If your child knows that she's expected to do her homework at a specific time every day, she will understand that homework is her first priority.

Work with your child to find the best time for homework. If possible, find a time that does not conflict with favorite activities, but make it clear that homework comes first. Homework time should be a time without interruptions and distractions, a time when your child's alert, and when someone can serve as a resource person.

While your child's at work, check in on her every fifteen minutes or so to offer help. Have her save questions until you come in, rather than ask them as they come up. Have her take a break every half hour or so (fifteen minutes for younger children). Five minutes away from a task can give her a fresh angle on it and can help her stay alert.

★ My Homework Schedule ★

Week of: Oct. 21

	Sunday	Monday	Tuesday	Wednesday	Thursday	Friday	Saturday
3:00		Snack	Snack	Computer Club	Snack	Scouts meeting ★	
3:30			homework	↓	home-work	↓	
4:00		home-work	soccer practice	Snack	soccer practice		
4:30				homework			
5:00					↓	★ ANNA'S	
5:30		↓	homework	↓	homework	SLEEP OVER	
6:00		dinner	dinner	dinner	dinner		
6:30				↓			
7:00		↓	↓	band concert	↓		
7:30							
8:00		bed	bed	↓	bed		
8:30		lights out	lights out	bed	lights out		
9:00						↓	

A homework schedule will help your child organize her time so that homework remains a priority.

4   Limit TV time.

Many experts recommend that children watch no more than ten hours of television (including videos) a week. By putting a limit on the time spent watching, you will make time available for more rewarding activities and for schoolwork.

Decide together how much television your child will watch. Have him list programs he wants to watch. From the choices, make a viewing schedule and stick to it.

Some families set a daily limit on total "screen time" (combined TV, computer, and video-game time). Consider making one day a week Z Day, for "Zero Screen-Time Day."

Provide alternatives to TV viewing, such as board games, books and magazines, and craft projects. Do *not* put a TV set in your child's room.

5 Use these magic words.

"I don't know." Don't give your child the answers. Finding the answer means learning to do research.

"Look it up." Sending her to a dictionary or almanac encourages the use of reference materials.

"Let's find out." Joining her in the search for information allows you to show her how it's done.

"What do you think?" Show her that you're interested in her thinking. She'll have to decide what she does think, and she'll have to state it clearly.

"Good job." When she does a good job, tell her so.

"Nice try." Nobody's perfect. She's not going to get everything right, but when she makes an honest effort, let her know that you recognize it and admire her for it.

6 Visit the library regularly.

Establish a routine of visiting the library. Make it a regular occurrence.

Resolving to go "soon" won't do, because "soon" is too likely to become "never." Instead, pick a day of the week and go to the library on that day every week—or at least every other week.

Get your child a library card so that he can take books out on his own.

When you and your child visit the library, borrow at least two books each. Make choosing books a pleasure, not a chore. Borrow books that interest you. Urge your child to do the same. Help him choose books by browsing among the new books, using the library catalog, and asking the librarian for suggestions.

Beyond the Basic Six

In this section you will find additional strategies for increasing the likelihood that your child will succeed in school.

These strategies are not listed in order of importance. Pick and choose from this selection of strategies as you would from a list of foods on a menu. Any selection you make is guaranteed to nourish your child's success in school.

7   Use calendars for planning.

Your child should have a calendar to keep track of school requirements. It's a good idea to keep a family calendar, too. The two calendars can work together to keep your child organized and focused.

The Family Calendar

Post a calendar where everyone in the family can use it. To keep track of individual activities, use a color code, with a color for each family member, and another for the entire family.

List family occasions, lessons, practices, medical appointments, and any other events that will cut into homework and study time.

List tests and major projects, such as book reports and research papers, so that family members will avoid scheduling conflicts.

FEBRUARY

Sunday	Monday	Tuesday	Wednesday	Thursday	Friday	Saturday
	1	Soccer 4-5 2	Band Rehearsal 3:30 3	Soccer 4-5 4	Band Concert 7PM 5	Ballet 9 a.m. 6
7	Early dismissal 11:45 8	Mom's Class 8-10 Soccer 4-5 9	10	Soccer 4-5 11	12	Ballet 9 a.m. 13
YOUTH GROUP 5:00 14	NO School 15	Mom's Class 8-10 Soccer 4-5 16	COUGAR REPORT DUE 17	W-dentist 4:45 Soccer 4-5 18	19	Ballet 9 a.m. 20
21	22	Mom's Class 8-10 Soccer 4-5 23	24	Soccer 4-5 25	ENERGY PROJECT DUE 26	Ballet 9 a.m. 27
28						

A family calendar will help everyone plan ahead and avoid scheduling conflicts.

Your Child's Calendar

For older children, a pocket organizer or assignment notebook is usually best. Dry-erase calendars or hand-drawn weekly calendars work well for younger ones.

Show your child how to use the calendar or assignment notebook to record homework, tests, and major projects.

Establish a daily time when you check your child's calendar and add any special school events or projects to the family calendar.

Older students need an assignment notebook to keep track of school assignments. Younger students can use a dry-erase board or hand-drawn calendars.

8 Do quick math drills.

Even in the age of palm-size computers, it is essential that your child learn math facts, such as multiplication tables. A child's ability to enjoy and excel in higher-level mathematics often depends on her facility with basic computation.

You can help with daily one-minute drills. Decide on a specific time for them, the same time every day. Give your child a sheet of math facts or a series of flash cards and note how many she can answer correctly in one minute. Don't spend more than a minute on these drills. You have to strike a delicate balance. On the one hand, your child has to build skill and speed, but too much time spent on drills may make her dislike math.

You can make minute-math work-sheets or flash cards, or you can buy drill workbooks, such as the *Minute Math Drills* series (see page 65), at an educational supply store or bookstore.

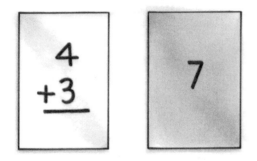

Help your child conquer math facts. Use a sheet of facts or flash cards to do quick one-minute math drills.

9   Establish a family reading night.

Once a week, set aside a quiet time when the whole family sits together in the same room and reads. Make reading the focus of the evening for everyone.

For yourself, choose something that you'll enjoy reading. If you find that you're not enjoying a book, choose another. Seeing you read for pleasure will encourage your child to read for pleasure.

If your child is reading longer chapter books, you may want to read your own copy of the book that she's reading. Then you'll be able to discuss the book together. Relax and enjoy the conversation.

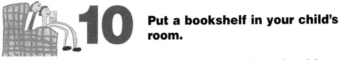

10 Put a bookshelf in your child's room.

Keep the shelf well stocked. It should include your child's own books, of course, but you can add to the stock and keep it fresh by including:

◆ books and magazines borrowed from the public library and your child's school library,
◆ books you and your child have swapped or borrowed from other families,
◆ free books and pamphlets from organizations,
◆ back issues of magazines passed along to you by friends and neighbors,
◆ bargain books from book clubs and used-book stores.

In addition, use the shelf to build a reference library for your child. Start with a dictionary.

11 Put a reading basket in the bathroom.

If your child reads more, she will soon read better. If she reads better, she will understand more of what she reads. If she understands more of what she reads, she will succeed in her school work.

The process begins with reading more, and any reading helps, including bath-room reading.

Magazines and catalogs make good bathroom reading. So do pamphlets and brochures. Some of the "junk mail" that comes into the house might go into the reading basket before it goes into the trash.

Be sure to keep the basket well stocked and replace materials regularly. Swap magazines with friends for more variety.

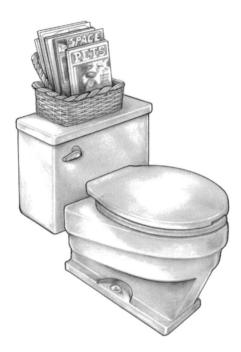

You can encourage reading simply by keeping reading materials in a convenient place like the bathroom.

12 Give books as gifts.

When you give someone a gift, you make two statements. You say that you care for the recipient, and you say that you value the gift itself.

If you give books as gifts, you'll demonstrate that you consider books valuable and enjoyable.

Involve your child in helping you choose gift books that suit the interests of the recipients. Together, look for books that are attractive, easy to read, fun to read, a pleasure to hold, and a pleasure to see.

Have giving in mind when you order from book clubs or visit book fairs.

Urge your child to make wish lists of books for birthday and holiday gifts, and make a gift-book wish list yourself.

13 Take your child to a reading or story hour.

To a beginning reader, a book can seem less glamorous and exciting than a television program or a movie. Books just lie there, after all. They don't move. They don't call out to us to read them.

Hearing a book read aloud can make reading a more personal experience. Meeting the author of a book can make books seem more glamorous and exciting. A signed copy of a book becomes a special object, and it can make the relationship between writing and reading more meaningful.

Bookstores and libraries often hold readings and story hours, which are usually free. Look for listings in your local newspaper or entertainment guide. Take the whole family.

14 Subscribe to a daily newspaper.

A daily newspaper is an obvious source of information about current events, but you can also use it as a teaching tool for virtually every academic area. For example:

- Math: sports statistics, business reports, graphs, ads (comparing prices)
- Science: science news, weather, technology news
- Social studies: maps, news of other countries
- Language arts: headlines (finding the main idea), crossword puzzles, comics (following a sequence)

Encourage your child to read the comic strips. Many a lifelong reader has begun that way.

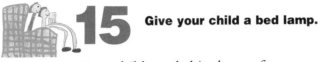

15 Give your child a bed lamp.

Your child needs his sleep, of course, especially on school nights, but he may not be ready for sleep at bedtime. Insist that the TV and stereo be turned off, but let him leave the lights on.

Get your child a bed lamp. If he shares the bedroom, get him a flashlight or a book light that will allow him to read without disturbing others.

Keep books and magazines on your child's bedside table. Good bedtime reading includes:

♦ high-interest magazines,
♦ books of short stories,
♦ chapter books that can be set aside at the end of a chapter and picked up again the next evening,
♦ old favorites, for their comfort value,
♦ picture books, which are easy for beginning readers and may be a welcome break for older readers.

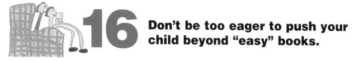

16 Don't be too eager to push your child beyond "easy" books.

To make your child an eager reader, don't push her into reading books that she may find too difficult. Let her take it easy.

Reading an easy book requires many of the skills that reading a hard book requires, but it doesn't seem like work. Picture books, in particular, can be a comfort and joy to readers of all ages.

For older readers, there are now many engagingly illustrated but conceptually sophisticated books available that will stretch both their reading abilities and their imaginations.

Don't discourage your child from reading the same books again and again. She'll go on to other books eventually. Meanwhile, she'll enjoy the comfort and success of rereading old favorites. That enjoyment will help make her a reader for life.

17 Limit extracurricular activities.

You know how you feel when it seems that there aren't enough hours in the day to do all the things that must be done— let alone the things you'd like to do. Your child can feel the same way. You'll be doing her a favor if you help her set priorities and limits. You'll also help to avoid (or at least alleviate) conflicts over how she should spend her time.

Begin by working together to make a chart showing the time available to her outside of school hours. Next, put onto the chart everything that must be done.

Begin with daily homework time and include meals, chores, and other family responsibilities.

When the "musts" are in place, your child will be able to see what free time is available to her. Have her list all the activities that she would like to pursue. Then have her decide which activity she most wants to do, and see how she can fit that into the schedule. Continue in decreasing priority until her time is filled.

If your child finds that she can't fit all the activities into the time available (which is likely), help her work out compromises, such as rescheduling in the next semester or season. Remind her that she has included the activities that she said she wanted most.

	Sunday	Monday	Tuesday	Wednesday	Thursday	Friday	Saturday
8:00			school	school	school	school	
9:00		school	school	school	school	school	soccer
10:00		school	school	school	school	school	soccer
11:00		school	school	school	school	school	soccer
12:00		school	school	school	school	school	
1:00		school	school	school	school	school	
2:00		school	school	school	school	school	soccer
3:00		piano	gymnastics	piano	library		
4:00		track team?	gymnastics	track team?		track team?	
5:00							
6:00	dinner	dinner	dinner	dinner	dinner	dinner	dinner
7:00		homework	homework	homework	homework	homework	
8:00	homework	homework	homework	homework	homework		
9:00	bed	bed	bed	bed	bed	bed	bed

Track meets are also on Saturday mornings! ☹

A chart showing after-school hours will help your child visualize the time that's available for extracurricular activities.

18 Establish a school-night routine.

To help your child complete his daily work and prepare for the next school day, establish a routine for school nights. Post a school-night checklist. Make sure that it includes:

♦ Finish homework and studying. This doesn't mean staying up late to finish; it means beginning early enough to finish.

♦ Check calendar for tomorrow to see what's coming up.

♦ See that everything is in place and ready to take to school tomorrow, including homework and permission slips.

♦ Go to bed early enough to get a good night's rest. This is especially important before a test. Staying up late to study is usually counter-productive.

A school-night checklist helps your child prepare for the next school day.

19 Establish a school-morning routine.

"Where's my shoe? Where's my backpack? What happened to my homework?" Chaos! It's no way to start the day.

To help your child—and yourself—begin the day calmly, establish a routine for school mornings.

Choose a place for your child to put all the things that she will have to take to school each morning. It should be someplace out of harm's way, such as a closet or the top of the refrigerator, so that the dog can't eat the homework and a younger sibling can't dismantle a project.

Help your child make up a school-morning checklist. Be sure the morning routine includes the following:

◆ Get up early enough to be ready without rushing.
◆ Eat breakfast.
◆ Check the backpack.

Before School

✓ Eat breakfast.
✓ Brush teeth.
✓ Check backpack:
    ✓ homework
    ✓ permission slip
    ✓ lunch money or lunch
    ✓ binder
    ✓ school books
    ✓ library books

A before-school checklist can help alleviate early morning panics.

20 Make breakfast interesting.

Study after study has shown that children do better in school if they eat breakfast than if they do not. They are more alert, think more clearly, and retain more of what they learn. For success in school, breakfast really is the most important meal of the day.

What your child eats for breakfast doesn't seem to matter. A peanut-butter-and-jelly sandwich or a square of leftover lasagna will work as well as bacon and eggs or a bowl of cereal.

So, expand your definition of breakfast to include some of your child's favorite foods, regardless of whether they fit your traditional definition of breakfast foods.

Good nutrition is important, of course, but you may want to indulge your child's whims to get him to eat the most important meal of the day.

21 Get your child a clock.

A watch is even better. If your child has a clock or watch, she will be able to keep herself on schedule. She'll know when it's time to end her play time and get settled into doing her homework. She'll begin to become responsible for her own schedule, for keeping appointments, and for budgeting her time.

When she's studying, she'll know when it's time to take a break. If she's taking a test in school, she'll know how much time remains, even if she's not at the best angle for seeing the clock on the classroom wall.

For some children, a clock or watch with a circular face is better than a digital one because it gives a graphic representation of the time in an hour, like a pie chart. For others, a digital display is easier to read. Choose the one that your child finds easier to follow.

22 Create a study space.

A special place for studying will give your child a sense of purpose—a sense of being at work, with a job to do.

For many children, the ideal is a study area in a quiet room, such as a bedroom. Wherever your child chooses to study, make sure that the area has a good light and a smooth, flat work surface.

If your child's study space is going to be the kitchen table, then create a kit of supplies (such as paper, pencils, and pens) and keep them together in a drawer, a covered box, or a sturdy shopping bag. At the start of study time, have the child set the space up for study the way you would set the table for dinner.

If more than one child needs study space, give each one an assigned place at the dining table or kitchen table.

Make sure that your child has a study area that is conducive to learning.

23 Buy your child a really cool pen.

Being a student is your child's profession.
Like any other profession, it requires a set
of tools. Good tools instill pride in the
profession, make doing the work much
more enjoyable, and make the work look
better. Be sure that your child has the
following:

- paper (loose-leaf paper or spiral note-books),
- pencils, pens, and crayons,
- a binder and folders in which to organize and preserve notes and work,
- as many other office supplies as you can provide, such as paper clips and a stapler, which make studying seem "official," and also lend a note of play to the work.

24   Give your child a dictionary.

A dictionary is the single most valuable reference work that you can have in the house.

If you can, get two dictionaries, a standard hardcover dictionary for the family and a smaller one—perhaps a paperback—for your child, or a picture dictionary for a younger child. Place a family dictionary in a central place.

To encourage use of the dictionary, get in the habit of saying "Look it up" when your child asks what a word means or how it is spelled. (You may have to help with this at first, but in time he should be able to find words and interpret dictionary entries on his own.)

25 Buy a globe.

The world is a big place, and for a child it can seem so big and diverse that it's impossible to grasp. A globe brings the world down to size. It turns the world into a place that your child can understand. A globe lets her hold the whole world in her hands. She can see how oceans, land masses, and countries are related to one another.

Use the family globe to find countries mentioned in the news. Use a piece of string to see how far places are from home. Compare the areas of distant lands with those that are more familiar, such as your home state.

Globes, maps, and atlases give different representations of the world. A globe is the best representation because it is the same shape as the real thing.

26 Help your child get organized.

If your child's backpack or book bag becomes a disorganized mess, urgent notices will sink to the bottom, never to be seen again, and his homework will arrive at school in tatters.

Help him get organized.

Begin by making a list of the types of things he will have to carry back and forth.

Next, assign each item to the best location, so that there's a place for everything and everything is in its place, for example:

- books and notebooks in the main compartment,
- homework papers in a sturdy folder in an inside pocket,
- supplies in zippered compartments and pockets,
- lunch in an outside compartment where books won't crush it.

Choose a special location for notices and notes sent back and forth between home and school. Help your child get into the habit of checking that location every afternoon when he arrives home from school and every morning before he leaves.

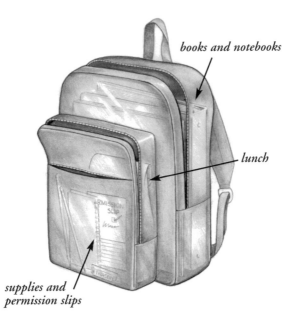

books and notebooks

lunch

supplies and permission slips

A well-organized backpack makes home-to-school transitions easier.

27 Set up a family message center.

To demonstrate the real-world value of writing and to help develop writing skills, establish a mail center that all family members can use. The refrigerator door is an ideal spot. Keep a small pad of paper in the kitchen. Use magnets to post messages. Dry-erase boards and self-stick notes also work well.

Use the message center to make writing part of the family's day-to-day communication in the following ways:

♦ Keep a while-you-were-out pad beside the telephone.
♦ Write notes to your child instead of giving oral instructions.
♦ Post a Menu Ideas sheet where everyone can list suggestions for upcoming meals.
♦ Post to-do lists for family members.
♦ Keep a running shopping list.

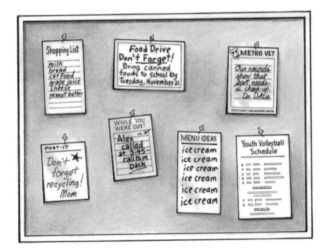

Use a family message center to make writing part of your daily communication.

28 Post a word of the day.

A family word of the day is a great vocabulary booster. You can simply post a word on the refrigerator door, but here's an approach that's more fun.

Write the word on a slip of paper for each family member. Each person's challenge is to learn about the word during the day and use it when you're together again. Slipping the word into conversation can become a game, and it can get quite hilarious.

You'll find many publications with word-of-the-day ideas, including calendars and notepads. You can find a word of the day online at the Web sites for Merriam-Webster (www.m-w.com) and Random House (www.randomhouse.com/wtod). You can also choose your own word of the day from the front page of the daily newspaper or your own dictionary.

29 Write letters.

Write letters, and encourage your child to write them, too. Letters demonstrate that writing is truly useful and that what your child writes has an effect on the person who reads it.

Sometimes you will be able to write letters together, and at other times you may want to have your child help you with your letters. Possibilities include:

- ◆ invitations and thank-you notes
- ◆ notes, letters, and postcards to relatives and friends
- ◆ mail orders
- ◆ fan letters
- ◆ requests for informative booklets, tourist brochures, and other items offered for free (see *Free Stuff for Kids* listed on page 65)
- ◆ notes and excuses for school (which you sign, of course)
- ◆ letters to the editor
- ◆ letters to a pen pal

30 Clip coupons.

So many coupons appear in magazines or in direct-mail advertising that they seem like a nuisance. To turn coupons into educational tools, have your child:

◆ choose and clip useful coupons (reasoning skills),
◆ categorize coupons into related groups, for example, by store or type of product (classifying skills),
◆ calculate savings (math skills),
◆ compare prices (math skills),
◆ read requirements for redeeming the coupon (critical reading skills).

31 Give your child a diary.

Did you keep a diary when you were a child? If you did, you probably remember the pleasure of having a place where you could write for yourself or to an imaginary friend, without having to worry about someone else's critical eye or red pen.

A diary encourages daily writing, of course, but it does many other good things for a child as well.

◆ It provides a place where a child can explore his thoughts, experiment with ideas, and develop a personal point of view.

◆ It helps him focus his thoughts and concentrate his attention.

◆ It provides an outlet for sorting out emotions and letting off steam.

32 Give your child a scrapbook.

Encourage your child to keep a scrapbook about herself, about someone whom she admires, or about a topic that interests her.

Keeping a scrapbook is fun, but there's more to it than that. It develops organizational skills and provides practice in classifying.

Building a scrapbook based on an interest may also lead to research and reading for information. Writing captions and comments teaches descriptive writing, accuracy, and succinctness.

If your child keeps a scrapbook about herself, she can use it as a portfolio of important school work. The book will help her see her progress, growth, and change. You will be able to use it to note her strengths and weaknesses and, if necessary, take steps to help her.

Keeping a scrapbook is fun and develops important organizational skills.

33 Play cards with your child.

After dinner, instead of watching television, play cards. Card games develop many skills that your child will need to succeed in school. For example:

◆ calculating and comparing values (War, Kings)
◆ recognizing sets (Go Fish, Crazy Eights, UNO®)
◆ sequencing (Gin Rummy, Spit, Solitaire)
◆ advance planning and strategic thinking
◆ weighing alternatives and making decisions
◆ fair play, cooperation, and following rules

The best source of rules and instructions for card games is *Hoyle's Rules of Games*, by Albert Morehead and Geoffrey Mott-Smith (New American Library).

34 Play board games with your child.

Board games make a great alternative to television. Playing a game gives you and your child time together and teaches him how to follow directions and play by the rules.

The best games are those that require thinking skills rather than those that depend entirely on chance. These games teach classification skills, strategic thinking, and pattern recognition.

- ◆ checkers, a simple game that's easy to learn
- ◆ go, an ancient game that takes just minutes to learn but a lifetime to master
- ◆ chess, difficult to learn, but unsurpassed as a thinking game
- ◆ Monopoly®, which teaches principles of investing and handling money

35 Play word games with your child.

It's no surprise that writers love word games. They really do make learning fun. Not only do word games increase your child's vocabulary and spelling ability, they also improve her ability to use words well. Consider enjoying some or all of the following with your child:

◆ crossword puzzles
◆ word search puzzles
◆ jumbles
◆ Scrabble®

You can find pencil-and-paper word games, such as crossword puzzles, in most daily newspapers. Many books of word games are available, too. A book of crossword puzzles can turn waiting times into learning times.

36 Teach math with money.

Money has a way of capturing attention. Harness this intriguing power of money and use it to build your child's interest in math. Each of the following routines can be financed with real money or with play money used as family scrip redeemable for treats or privileges.

♦ Give your child an allowance or pay her for specific jobs.
♦ Help her work out a budget.
♦ Give your child an account book (ledger) to keep track of income and expenses.
♦ Help her open a bank account.
♦ If your child seems ready, introduce her to the stock market. Have her "buy" stocks on paper, follow them in the daily newspaper's stock market tables, and make investment decisions.

37 Take monthly family field trips.

Broaden your child's horizons. Chances are good that he knows as much as he needs to know about popular culture. Introduce him to aspects of culture that he would not encounter otherwise.

Make a monthly date for an educational or cultural field trip. Mark the date on the family calendar. Try some of these:

◆ zoos, botanical gardens, and aquariums
◆ art museums
◆ science museums and natural history museums
◆ concerts
◆ theatrical performances
◆ historical sites

38

Teach your child how to . . .

Teach your child how to do something that you know how to do. It might be how to cook or how to do carpentry or how to sew. The specific skill that you teach her is not as important as the time you spend together and the many lessons she will learn along the way.

In the process of baking bread, building a fence, or making a quilt, your child will learn how to learn. She'll learn to focus her attention, follow directions, be precise, and distinguish essential details from unimportant ones.

As you teach her, be alert for "teachable moments." These are opportunities to teach basic facts and skills, such as making measurements or calculating fractions, that are useful in almost any area. You'll find that these teachable moments will come up in the teaching of any skill.

39 **Save your child's schoolwork.**

Work with your child to establish an archive of his schoolwork.

Throughout the year, help your child choose homework papers, tests, book reports, and projects to save.

Accordion file folders are a good choice for organizing the papers. Categorizing the work will teach your child organizational skills, and the files can be a great help in studying. When he's given an assignment, have him look through the files to find similar assignments that will help him with the new work.

At the start of a new school year, go through last year's file. Discuss the work as you do so. Look for patterns of strength and weakness. Praise his strengths and work together to set goals for improvement in the coming year.

40

Find something to praise.

Would you rather be praised for something you did well or criticized for something you did badly? It's an easy choice, isn't it?

Too often, children hear more criticism than praise for the schoolwork they do. That can be discouraging. (Think how different the situation is in baseball, where a .400 hitter is an all-star, even though she doesn't get a hit most of the time.)

Learn to look for the good things that your child does. Post good work where everyone can see it. Thank her for helping you when she does. If she spells most of the words in an essay correctly, praise that fact before you point out the words she misspelled.

Children learn quickly that empty praise is manipulative. Praise genuinely and appropriately.

41

Stay in touch with your child's teacher.

When the school year begins, introduce yourself to your child's teacher. Explain that you want to stay in touch by phone, note, or E-mail.

On a calendar, mark dates for check-ins at intervals of two or three weeks. At the very least, check in with the teacher two-thirds of the way through each marking period. You'll have the last third of the period to overcome problems. If your child's behavior or attitude changes, contact the teacher immediately.

Thank your child's teacher when you check in. You might mention new understandings your child has attained with the teacher's help. Teachers often hear complaints; a little praise can go a long way.

42 Don't . . .

. . . insist that your child finish a book that he is reading for pleasure. If he doesn't like it or finds it too difficult, encourage him to choose another. (Do insist that he finish school assignments, though.)

. . . make him read aloud if he's reluctant to do so.

. . . do his homework for him.

. . . put a television set in your child's bedroom.

. . . let stress get out of hand. If your child seems overly anxious about school work, confer with his teacher to see what can be done.

. . . lose track of what's happening in your child's school life. Ask him about his schoolwork.

. . . criticize your child in front of others.

43 Do . . .

. . . read with your child as often as possible.

. . . visit the library with your child, and make it a habit.

. . . use calendars and organizers to help your child stay organized.

. . . maintain homework time, not to be interrupted by other activities.

. . . keep your child's television viewing to a minimum.

. . . praise your child in front of others.

. . . establish routines for school nights and school mornings.

. . . return to this book from time to time to see what additional strategies you might adopt.

Six Books for Reading Aloud

These anthologies offer a wide range of literature. When you find what you and your child enjoy, look for similar titles in Jim Trelease's *Read-Aloud Handbook.*

- *Classics to Read Aloud to Your Children*, edited by William Russell
- *The Great Lives* series, edited by William Jacobs
- *Hey! Listen to This*, edited by Jim Trelease
- *The People Could Fly: American Black Folktales* by Virginia Hamilton
- *A Treasury of Children's Literature*, edited by Armand Eisen
- *The 20th-Century Children's Book Treasury*, edited by Janet Schulman

Ten High-Interest Books
That Are Easy to Read

- *Abel's Island* by William Steig
- The *Bunnicula* series by Deborah and James Howe
- *Catwings* by Ursula K. Le Guin
- *Cricket in Times Square* by George Seldon
- *How to Eat Fried Worms* by Thomas Rockwell
- *The Littles* series by John Peterson
- *Mr. Popper's Penguins* by Richard and Florence Atwater
- *Pippi Longstocking* by Astrid Lindgren
- *The Random House Book of Easy-to-Read Stories*
- *Wolf Story* by William McCleery

Ten Stimulating Picture Books

- *Earth from Above* by Yann Arthus-Bertrand
- *Eating Fractions* by Bruce McMillan
- *Eye to Eye* by Frans Lanting
- *The 500 Hats of Bartholomew Cubbins* by Dr. Seuss
- *How Are You Peeling?* by Saxton Freymann and Joost Elffers
- *Look-Alikes* by Joan Steiner
- *The New Way Things Work* by David Macauley
- *The Polar Express* by Chris Van Allsburg
- *Sector 7* by David Weisner
- *The Stinky Cheeseman and Other Fairly Stupid Tales* by Jon Scieszka

Ten Chapter Books

- *The Black Stallion* by Walter Farley
- *Charlotte's Web* by E. B. White
- *The Chronicles of Narnia* by C. S. Lewis
- *Homer Price* by Robert McCloskey
- *The Indian in the Cupboard* by Lynne Reid Banks
- *James and the Giant Peach* by Roald Dahl
- *Just So Stories* by Rudyard Kipling
- The *Little House* series by Laura Ingalls Wilder
- The *Ramona* series by Beverly Cleary
- *The Wind in the Willows* by Kenneth Grahame

Seven Books for You

- *Family Math* by Stenmark, Thompson, and Cossey
- *Free Stuff for Kids* (Meadowbrook Press)
- The *Minute Math Drills* series (Carson-Deliosa Publishing)
- *The New York Times Parents' Guide to the Best Books for Children* by Eden Ross Lipson
- *Raising a Reader* by Paul Kropp
- *The Read-Aloud Handbook* by Jim Trelease
- *The 7 Habits of Highly Effective Families* by Stephen R. Covey

Five Web Sites for You

- Children First
  www.pta.org
  (National Parent-Teachers Association)
- The *New York Times* Learning
  Network
  www.nytimes.com/learning
  (New York Times)
- Home Page for Parents and Caregivers
  www.ala.org/alsc/parents.links.html
  (Association for Library Service to
  Children)
- Helping Children Succeed in School
  www.urbanext.uiuc.edu/succeed/
  (University of Illinois Extension/
  University of Illinois at Urbana-
  Champaign)
- Helping Your Child
  www.ed.gov/pubs/parents/hyc.html
  (U. S. Department of Education)

Small Books are packed with helpful ideas and useful strategies—creating more effective classrooms and more successful students! Order yours today!

Two easy ways to order:

Web: **www.renlearn.com/3**

By Phone: **(800) 338-4204, ref. #4948S**

Renaissance
Learning™

Valuable Resources for Teachers and Parents!

These four Small Books contain big ideas! *44 Routines That Make a Difference* and *Life-Saving Strategies for New Teachers* offer great tips and techniques for teachers. Parents will love the simple ideas in *Help Your Child Succeed in School* and *How to Help With Homework*—both available in Spanish!

⚙ **44 Routines That Make a Difference**
ISBN 1-893751-61-9
Item #TS96-3088

⚙ **Life-Saving Strategies for New Teachers**
ISBN 1-893751-88-0
Item #TS96-3147

⚙ **Help Your Child Succeed in School**
ISBN 1-893751-80-5
Item #TS96-3133

⚙ **Cómo ayudar a su niño a tener éxito en la escuela**
ISBN 1-893751-92-9
Item #TS96-3149

⚙ **How To Help with Homework**
ISBN 1-893751-84-8
Item #TS96-3142

⚙ **Cómo ayudar con las tareas escolares**
ISBN 1-893751-89-9
Item #TS96-3151

Each book is only $8.95.

> **SAVE! Mix and match—buy 10 or more of any Small Books and pay only $7.95 each!**

Small Books are easy to order—
turn the page for complete details!